Concrete Sea

EA Giffiths

Cinnamon Press
:: small miracles from distinctive voices ::

Published by Cinnamon Press
Office 49019, PO Box 15113, Birmingham, B2 2NJ.
www.cinnamonpress.com

The right of EA Griffiths to be identified as author of this work has been asserted by her in accordance with the Copyright, Designs and Patent Act, 1988. © 2023, EA Griffiths.

ISBN 978-1-78864-140-1

British Library Cataloguing in Publication Data. A CIP record for this book can be obtained from the British Library.

All rights reserved. No part of this publication may be reproduced, stored in a retrieval system, or transmitted in any form or by any means, electronic, mechanical, photocopying, recording or otherwise without the prior written permission of the publishers. This book may not be lent, hired out, resold or otherwise disposed of by way of trade in any form of binding or cover other than that in which it is published, without the prior consent of the publishers.

Designed and typeset in Bodoni by Cinnamon Press. Cover design by Adam Craig.

Cinnamon Press is represented by Inpress Ltd.

Contents

Angel	9
Seabed	10
Sea Song	11
B)d(	12
Breath/Anadl	13
Walking in front of the hearse at a funeral	14
So many pieces of my heart are broken	15
The Suit	16
Conversation	17
E-mail	18
The Rhondda	19
Abacus	20
Shock	21
Woman in a Broken Mirror	22
The Morning After	23
Cydymaith	24
The Beach	25
Cyfrifiad 2021	26
Rhondda 1900	27
Jacob Price	28
Triawd yn Canu ar Lwyfan yr Eisteddfod / Trio Singing on the Eisteddfod Stage	29
The Skull	30
Blodeuwedd 2019	31
Piano	32
writing	33
Castell Nos (standing above The Rhondda)	34
Flower	35
Emyn yn y Capel / A Hymn in Chapel	36
Miscarriage	37
Worship	38
and i am turning the	39
Notes	40

I Dad cariad A

Concrete Sea

Angel

And when
you
touched
my hip
it was
the
familiar
story
of bone,
socket,
light.

Seabed

And we sat
on the
soft bed
of the ocean
spinning
our tales
of nacre
into a
bright
shimmering
pearl.

Sea Song

I have buried
my voice
in the green sea,
in the pink ear
of a shell,
in the long,
piercing note
of a ship
deserted
on the rocks.

B)d(

            &   w'nt

              p(t''ll

                   ;:'

           h+>.   t-

p/^nf|lw   ~~wr!t~~"

=t   th^s

}sb   b~d}

Breath/Anadl

[h]   [h]   [h]   [h]   [h]   [h]   [h]
   [h]   [h]   [h]   [h]   [h]   [h]
[h]   [h]   [h]   [h]   [h]   [h]   [h]
   [h]   [h]   [h]   [h]   [h]   [h]
[h]   [h]   [h]   [h]   [h]   [h]   [h]
   [h]   [h]   [h]   [h]   [h]   [h]
[h]   [h]   [h]   [h]   [h]   [h]   [h]
   [h]   [h]   [h]   [h]   [h]   [h]
[h]   [h]   [h]   [h]   [h]   [h]   [h]
   [h]   [h]   [h]   [h]   [h]   [h]
[h]   [h]   [h]   [h]   [h]   [h]   [h]
   [h]   [h]   [h]   [h]   [h]   [h]
[h]   [h]   [h]   [h]   [h]   [h]   [h]
   [h]   [h]   [h]   [h]   [h]   [h]
[h]   [h]   [h]   [h]   [h]   [h]   [h]
   [h]   [h]   [h]   [h]   [h]   [h]
[h]   [h]   [h]   [h]   [h]   [h]   [h]
   [h]   [h]   [h]   [h]   [h]   [h]
[h]   [h]   [h]   [h]   [h]   [h]   [h]
   [h]   [h]   [h]   [h]   [h]   [h]
[h]   [h]   [h]   [h]   [h]   [h]   [h]
[h]   [h]   [h]   [h]   [h]   [h]   [h]   [h]

Walking in front of the hearse at a funeral

step
step
step
step
step
step
step
step
step
step
step
step
step
step
step
step
step
step
step
step
step
step
step
step
step
step
step
step
step
step
step
step
step
step
step
step
step

So many pieces of my heart are broken

                                                                                   my

so   pieces

              many   heart

                           broken   of

are

                                                                   of

            so

                              pieces

                                                                        so

                        many

heart   are

                                                               broken

my

           many   are

                     pieces

                                             heart

of

           broken

                                                        my

The Suit

Jacket,
tie,
shirt
written
last night
in your
diary
and pulled
this morning
letter
by letter
across
your
frame.

Conversation

Silence
golden
a child
between us -
I can hear
your legs
thudding
back
to roundabouts
swung by
the wind
and a mother's
shaking finger
over the
camera lens.
That shadow
on your chest,
the one that
presses down
and folds
the skin into
a cupped hand,
it is there
that I can
listen to
your heart
pressed up
to the rib cage
a dead bird.

E-mail

I sent,
you sent,
words tumbling
old-fashioned springs
coiling and uncoiling
across the screen,
taking me back
through the trail
of your thoughts
away from the
white heat
of an argument
to the still,
quiet genesis
of your point.

The Rhondda

orange
river
of my
heart

Abacus

We are
counting
the days
to leave,
halving
multiplying
the hours
with the
bright
algorithm
of beads.

Shock

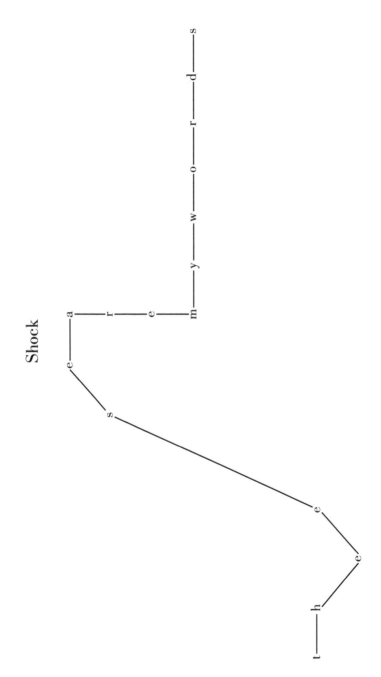

Woman in a Broken Mirror

       d   a e h

          d na   h

     t   sa   erb

            m r a

The Morning After

Your body
dragged out
of bed
a layer
of skin
from a bruised knee
night,
morning,
afternoon
stirred,
mixed,
sloshing
in your head
a whiskey chaser.

th

i

a

m

y

d

y

c

The Beach

Today, if I put
the sea
to my ear
a shell,
I can hear
a thousand
of your journeys
hitting the shore,
feel the sand
pulling me
through
its grains
to a kingdom
of lost children
and hastily built
sandcastles.

Cyfrifiad 2021

Cwestiwn 17

Rhondda 1900

fog
and
a shrill
red
note
calls
the
valley
to dust

Jacob Price

Jacob Price,
I am calling you out
from your tea and toast
and the counting
of oranges
and lemons
in their green
net coats
into the
stripped glare
of the shop floor
and bright groceries
parading their stickers
at the end of the day.
Jacob Price,
I am calling you,
come.

Triawd yn Canu ar Lwyfan yr Eisteddfod /
Trio Singing on the Eisteddfod Stage

....

> >

****

....

> >

****

....

> >

****

....

> >

****

....

> >

****

....

> >

****

....

> >

****

....

> >

****

The Skull

50, 13, 48, 1
2, 14, 5 , 2
0, 14, 2
3, 18
1
,
4
1
4,
6, 2
,43 ,1
1:50 lef
t eye, chi
n, crown, tim
e. ... E.A. Griffiths

Blodeuwedd 2019

Gwydion
made
her
this
time
from
salt,
car
lights
and
pearls.

Piano

Open
the lid—
there are
notes
humming
a soft
tune—
curling
a bright
flower
around
my wrist.

writing

and I
am
sick
with
images
and light

Castell Nos (standing above The Rhondda)

heather
coal
shining
purple
crumbling
through
castle walls
brittle
with
whinberries
and stone.

Flower

This
flower
closes
the door
on the
bright
yellow
of sunshine.

Emyn yn y Capel / A Hymn in Chapel

ffdd gbth crd pr hdd ffdd gbth crd pr hdd ffdd gbth crd pr hdd ffdd
gbth crd pr hdd ffdd gbth crd pr hdd ffdd gbth crd pr hdd ffdd gbth
crd pr hdd ffdd gbth crd pr hdd ffdd gbth crd pr hdd ffdd gbth crd pr
hdd ffdd gbth crd pr hdd ffdd gbth crd pr hdd ffdd gbth crd pr hdd
ffdd gbth crd pr hdd ffdd gbth crd pr hdd ffdd gbth crd pr hdd ffdd
gbth crd pr hdd ffdd gbth crd pr hdd ffdd gbth crd pr hdd ffdd gbth
crd pr hdd ffdd gbth crd pr hdd ffdd gbth crd pr hdd ffdd gbth crd pr
hdd ffdd gbth crd pr hdd ffdd gbth crd pr hdd ffdd gbth crd pr hdd
ffdd gbth crd pr hdd ffdd gbth crd pr hdd ffdd gbth crd pr hdd ffdd
gbth crd pr hdd ffdd gbth crd pr hdd ffdd gbth crd pr hdd ffdd gbth
crd pr hdd ffdd gbth crd pr hdd ffdd gbth crd pr hdd ffdd gbth crd pr
hdd ffdd gbth crd pr hdd ffdd gbth crd pr hdd ffdd gbth crd pr hdd
ffdd gbth crd pr hdd ffdd gbth crd pr hdd ffdd gbth crd pr hdd ffdd
gbth crd pr hdd ffdd gbth crd pr hdd ffdd gbth crd pr hdd ffdd gbth
crd pr hdd ffdd gbth crd pr hdd ffdd gbth crd pr hdd ffdd gbth crd pr
hdd ffdd gbth crd pr hdd ffdd gbth crd pr hdd ffdd gbth crd pr hdd
ffdd gbth crd pr hdd ffdd gbth crd pr hdd ffdd gbth crd pr hdd ffdd
gbth crd pr hdd ffdd gbth crd pr hdd ffdd gbth crd pr hdd ffdd gbth
crd pr hdd ffdd gbth crd pr hdd ffdd gbth crd pr hdd ffdd gbth crd pr
hdd ffdd gbth crd pr hdd ffdd gbth crd pr hdd ffdd gbth crd pr hdd
ffdd gbth crd pr hdd ffdd gbth crd pr hdd ffdd gbth crd pr hdd ffdd
gbth crd pr hdd ffdd gbth crd pr hdd ffdd gbth crd pr hdd ffdd gbth
crd pr hdd ffdd gbth crd pr hdd ffdd gbth crd pr hdd ffdd gbth crd pr
hdd ffdd gbth crd pr hdd ffdd gbth crd pr hdd ffdd gbth crd pr hdd
ffdd gbth crd pr hdd ffdd gbth crd pr hdd ffdd gbth crd pr hdd ffdd
gbth crd pr hdd ffdd gbth crd pr hdd ffdd gbth crd pr hdd ffdd gbth
crd pr hdd ffdd gbth crd pr hdd ffdd gbth crd pr hdd ffdd gbth crd pr
hdd ffdd gbth crd pr hdd ffdd gbth crd pr hdd ffdd gbth crd pr hdd
ffdd gbth crd pr hdd ffdd gbth crd pr hdd ffdd gbth crd pr hdd ffdd

Miscarriage

Worship

light
mirror
flame

and a miniam turning the

Notes

'The Skull' (p. 32): Numbers drawn from a plastic model of a human skull used to teach students of anatomy.

'Emyn yn y Capel / A Hymn in Chapel' (p. 38): The words (with vowels removed) are from the hymn 'Gwahoddiad' (ffydd, gobaith, cariad pur a hedd—faith, hope, pure love and peace). They are laid over a transcription of a recording of a church congregation chatting after a Sunday service.

Lightning Source UK Ltd.
Milton Keynes UK
UKHW012049210223
417406UK00005B/391